Morton Gould

Suite
for Violin and Piano

Piano

ED-3907
First Printing: October 1993

G. SCHIRMER, Inc.

DISTRIBUTED BY
HAL•LEONARD®
CORPORATION
7777 W. BLUEMOUND RD. P.O. BOX 13819 MILWAUKEE, WI 53213

Suite for Violin and Piano
(1945)

By MORTON GOULD (1945)
Edited by Max Pollikoff

1. Warm Up

Playing time 2:15

Driving

2. Serenade

Playing time 4:50

on the fingerboard

Gayer—a bit faster

9

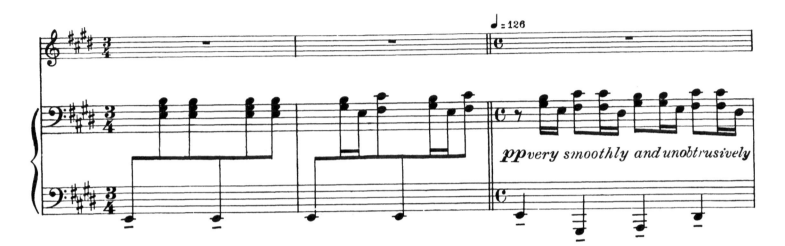

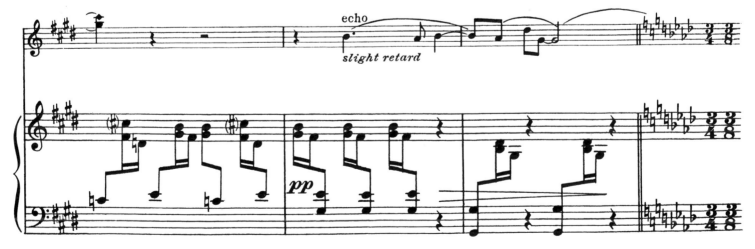

3. March

Playing time 3:00

MORTON GOULD

Brisk and well-marked ♩=112
With rowdy gusto

Quarter
tone bend.

fading away

bring out

ppp

ppp

Morton Gould

Suite
for Violin and Piano

Violin

ED-3907
First Printing: October 1993

G. SCHIRMER, Inc.

DISTRIBUTED BY

HAL•LEONARD®
CORPORATION
7777 W. BLUEMOUND RD. P.O. BOX 13819 MILWAUKEE, WI 53213

Suite for Violin and Piano

Violin

By MORTON GOULD (1945)
Edited by Max Pollikoff

1. Warm Up

Bright driving tempo ♩= 152
Well marked hard-bitten thru-out
Heavily on the string

2. Serenade

Violin

3. March

Violin

MORTON GOULD

Brisk and well marked ♩=112
With rowdy gusto

clipped **f**

short

fading away

* Quarter tone bend

ff on the string
attack

tr ponticello

pp

tr

tr

tr

tr

ponticello

p

4. Blues

Violin

5. Hoe Down

Violin

MORTON GOULD

on the string

4. Blues

Playing time 5:30

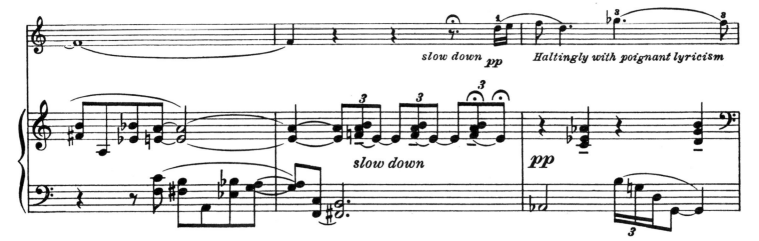

slow down *pp*   *Haltingly with poignant lyricism*

slow down   *pp*

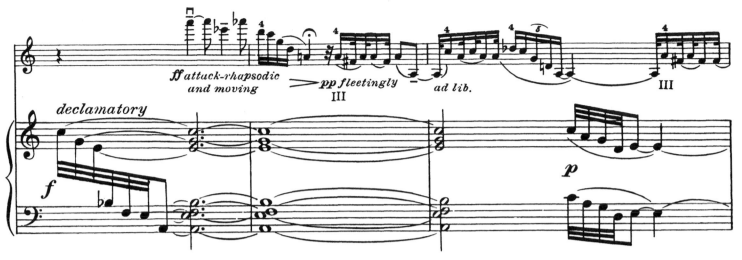

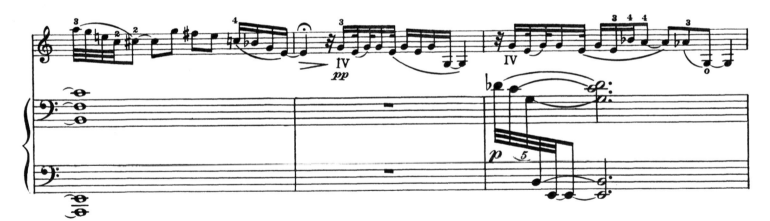

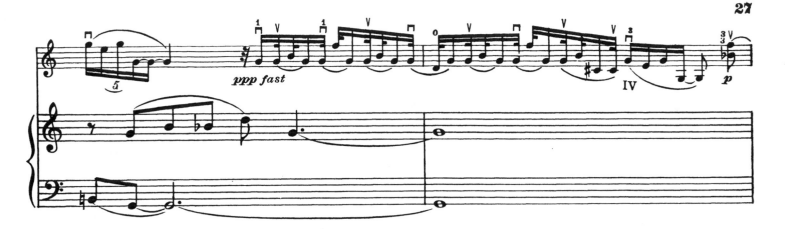

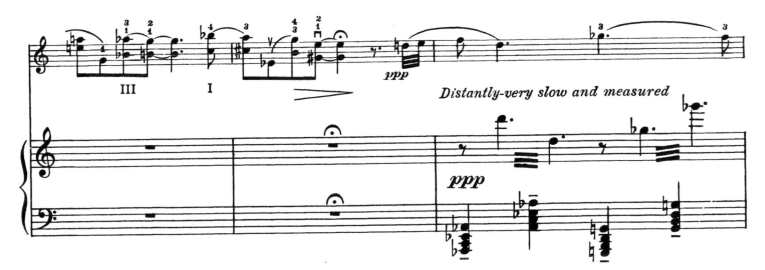

On the fingerboard

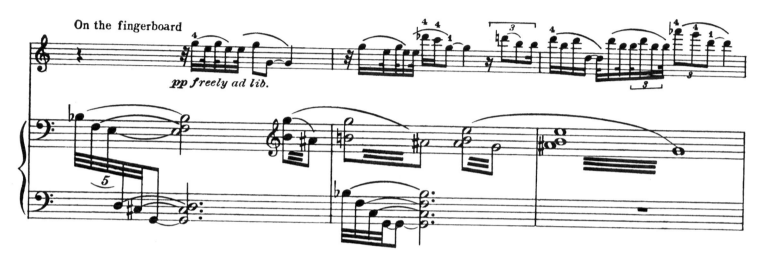

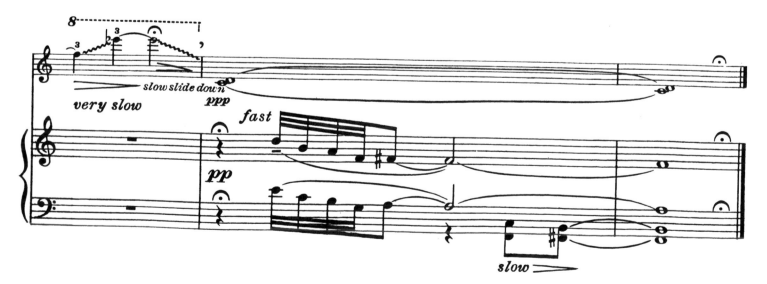

5. Hoe Down

Playing time 2:30

MORTON GOULD

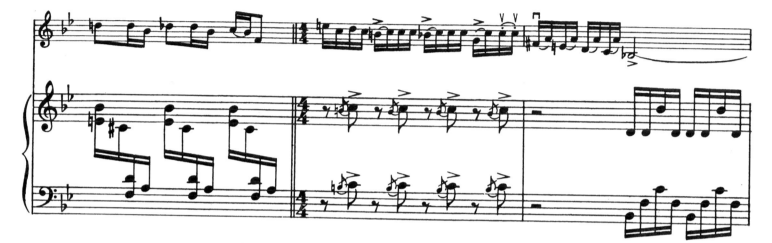

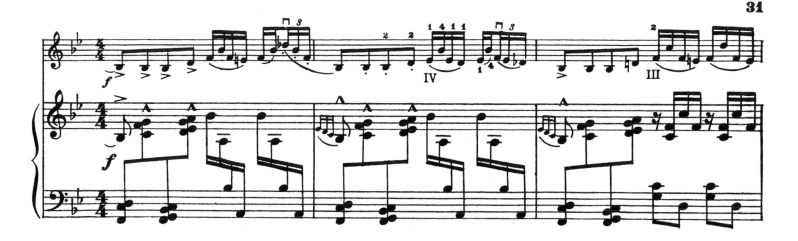